Distributed By
CARSON ENTERPRISES
801 Juniper Ave.
Boulder, Colo. 80302

Jim Bowie's
Lost Mine

Jim Bowie's
Lost Mine

by
M. E. FRANCIS

The Naylor Company
Book Publishers of the Southwest
San Antonio, Texas

Originally published under the title
BOWIE'S LOST MINE, 1954

Second Printing 1958

Third Printing 1962

JIM BOWIE'S LOST MINE

Second Edition, Revised and Enlarged, 1966

Second Printing 1970

Distributed By
CARSON ENTERPRISES
P. O. DRAWER 71
DEMING, N. MEX. 88030

TO

MYNNIE   WILLIAMS   SCHENKENBERG

Whose life, like the wide skies of Texas, had ever brightened, shielded and blessed her land. She was devoted to Texas in its varied beauty, its stirring traditions and its distinctive ideals.
She was as friendly as the wide Texas
skies, as serenely inspiring as its
Alamo.

FOREWORD

In this story of *Jim Bowie's Lost Mine,* history and legend meet and mingle. I have written the tale as the hunters for the elusive treasure and frontiersmen of an early day have handed it down. Thousands of Texans believed then, and others still believe, that the mine exists. The search to find it still goes on!

The descriptive ceremonials, dances and social customs of the Indians used in this narrative have been recast after careful research regarding the life and customs of the aborigines in early pioneer days while Texas was still a part of Mexico.

M. E. FRANCIS

CONTENTS

1 First Sign of Adventure   13

2 The Lost Mine   19

3 A Trip to Mexico   31

4 A Campfire Agreement   43

5 Gifts for the Chief   48

6 Adoption by the Tribe   54

7 A Good Indian   60

8 Return to San Antonio   66

9 A Fight with Tres Manos   70

10 A Search for the Mine   76

11 The Calf Creek Battle   82

12 The Last Fight   88

LIST OF ILLUSTRATIONS

Frontispiece   ii

Jim left the smithy and rode toward the inn.   29

Holding her close, Jim promised he would return.   39

Jim revealed a rifle with a silver name-plate.   51

Tres Manos caught Jim in the chest with his head.   73

1

First Sign of Adventure

*T*HE soft, caressing Texas breeze suddenly changed into a cold, penetrating gale. Heavy storm clouds banked across the western sky, obscuring the afterglow of a September sunset. Torrents of rain, borne on the wind of a howling norther, swept through the streets of frontier San Antonio, drenching a hapless wayfarer and forcing him to seek shelter wherever it could be found.

The horseman, leading his mount, emerged from the night's sudden blackness and strode into the cheery shelter of Pete Bauer's blacksmith shop.

13

The newcomer was a well-built, distinguished-looking young man whose vibrant muscularity was confirmed by his every movement. You were not impressed by his height until you saw him towering above the sturdy form of the blacksmith. His wavy, auburn hair sprang impatiently away from his high forehead, only to dip low again in narrow, neatly-barbered sideburns.

In a rich, mellow voice he introduced himself: "Howdy, sir. My name is Bowie — James Bowie. I'm a stranger in these parts. While riding in from the hill country this afternoon, my horse lost a shoe. Can your man reshoe the filly while I enjoy the shelter of your shop and wait for the fury of this storm to spend itself?"

Wiping his hands on his leather apron, Bauer came forward. "You're right welcome here, stranger," he responded as he shook hands and waved Bowie to a seat on a bench before the open fire. He called, "Sambo! Take the gentleman's horse; see that she's rubbed down and reshod."

This done, the genial proprietor returned to his guest and settled down to enjoy the evening. "Your horse will be well cared for, sir, and I'm grateful for a chance to serve you, for business

14

is slack these days. The prospect of welcoming a new neighbor affords me pleasure. I take it you came down to look Texas over," remarked old Pete. "Well, son, she's a great country! I came down myself with Steve Austin's colony, hoping to improve my fortune, and I've never regretted the move.

"Most of our first settlers were thrifty, God-fearing men and women who came as pioneers wanting to have a part in building up our new country. Some came for adventure and some for other reasons, but they've all done well. Even the floaters who drifted in without enough spare duds to dust a banjo have improved their condition, too! Some of them have even pre-empted land, built 'dobe houses, rustled up a string of cattle, married fine girls, settled down and are doing well.

"You see, sir, just the name Texas acts like a lodestone. It attracts daring young men, draws them within her borders and holds them, just as a strong magnet attracts and holds steel filings — or as clover fields in early summer entice and satisfy honeybees. Yes, sir, whether these young men come for adventure or other reasons, nearly all of them like it here and stay.

"Once the young fellows are here, they want

15

to sink their roots deep into the virgin soil and become a part of this — our great, virile, throbbing new state. Seems like there's always a hidden secret, or an unsatisfied ambition that draws men to Texas. I often think how interesting it would be to know the inside story about some of these aggressive young blades," concluded old Pete.

"I find high adventure in business," rejoined Bowie genially. "I came to Texas on an exploratory expedition. I want to see a lot of country before I settle down anywhere — but the more I see of Texas, the better I like what she has to offer.

"Are the Indians hereabouts troublesome? I met a band of them riding at top gallop this afternoon, just before the storm broke. Their leader was no ordinary-looking man. From his trappings, the way he rode his horse and handled himself, he seemed to me to be a man of rank among his tribesmen. You should have seen him! He gave me a friendly 'How' in passing."

"That must have been Old Chief Xolic and his head tribesmen. Reckon I've seen him a hundred times or more. He's the chief and high sachem of the Lipan Indian tribe. They live out in the hills of Liltamilpas and guard the secret of the lost mine," responded old Pete.

"I've heard tall tales about Spanish grandees who have buried their treasure to keep it from falling into the hands of crafty rulers," said Jim. "But a lost mine intrigues me! That really is too fantastic!"

"Yes, I reckon it might seem strange, 'specially to a newcomer," mused Pete. "But the mine is out there somewhere, just the same; the ill-fated Almagres mine is surely tucked away up there in the San Saba hills. But it's not at all likely any white man will ever live to find it and take out the ore — though they do say he would be rich as Croesus if he could."

"That is an amazing statement, Mr. Bauer. Why do you really think there is such a mine? What evidence do you have to back up such a claim?" Bowie put the question skeptically.

"Oh, there's plenty of bona fide evidence all right," countered Pete. "I'll start with Sam Fordney. He keeps the trading post store. Sam says that when those Lipan Indians come into his store to trade, they nearly always have lizard-shaped nuggets of pure silver to pay for as much duffle as they want to take away. They are always well-supplied with nuggets, but where they come from is a tribal secret, and not a living redskin will ever answer any questions put to him about it.

"But there's trouble in the wind among the Indians themselves now. The old chief is an honest old hombre who wants to live at peace with the white settlers, but Xolic is getting old. His children are all girls; he has no son to carry on for him and keep the young bucks in line, so a rift has developed among the Indians themselves.

"There's a young set of hoodlums who won't listen to the old chief's council. They're led by a crafty young warrior — Tres Manos — who's always looking for some excuse to strike the post and go on the warpath against the palefaces. His followers are a surly, suspicious lot, always trying to ferret out or start real trouble," concluded old Pete.

2

The Lost Mine

JIM produced a plug of tobacco from a pouch, shaved down a handful, tamped it into the bowl of his pipe, lighted it with a live coal, which he deftly took from the embers on the hearth, and smoked reflectively.

After a short silence he remarked: "You say there really *is* a lost mine, eh? The idea intrigues me. But first I'd like to know why such a prize has been so long neglected and the search for it abandoned. Do you, sir, honestly believe there's a paying mine yonder in those hills?

"Might it not be that this legend of a lost

mine is only a Spanish myth — a will-o'-the-wisp which beguiles men's souls, fires their imagination, stimulates their ambition — but leads them nowhere! I have a yen to know the reason for lack of interest in the lost mine. Will you explain the mystery of this lost mine? There must be some powerful force holding the gold-diggers back. What is it?"

"So you, too, want the story of the Almagres mine," mused Pete. "Well, sir, it's a tale of wild unrest — a chronicle of human acts as turbulent and unrestrained as the storm that just rode in on the winds of this norther! Yes, sir, the tantalizing urge to find that lost mine has caused many an ardent young chap — and older men, too — to go out hunting it. But each one, in turn, bit the dirt on a lonely trail, with only the dismal howl of coyotes to announce his passing!

"Well, sir — this is the story: The Almagres mine was discovered by an itinerant Spanish padre while doing missionary work among the Indians about the middle of the last century. The priest was also a geologist, so he carried specimens of ore back to Mexico City. There the rocks were tested and found to be rich in silver. The government lost no time in clinching its claims. Other and more comprehensive surveys were ordered.

"The missionary padre, accompanied by other priests, engineers commissioned as Army officers and soldiers, soon returned to the San Saba region. There, with the help of some converted Indians, a strong, spacious mission was built. The buildings were ample to house all officers, soldiers and mine-workers, as well as the missionaries and their attendants.

"The spacious quarters were enclosed by triple rows of palisading, while four cannons, trained on the entrance to the mine, were mounted on the broad, sturdy gate posts.

"Soon after, the Spanish-born promoters opened the mine and had it operating full-blast. After the first few loads of smelted ore were run through, reports of the mine's exceeding richness and enormous yield spread like wildfire. The rumor brought in ruffians of the very worst type. They were as bloody a lot of pirates as ever set foot on virgin soil.

"These scoundrels carried things through in a mighty high-handed way. They abused the mission Indians, robbed their gardens and slaughtered their flocks. They drove the able-bodied redskins into the mine with cat-o'-nine-tails and made them dig out the ore. No galley slave-driver ever made slaves work harder than those roughnecks did the captive Indians.

"After forcing the arrogant, nature-loving red men to work underground all day, the soldiers herded the poor devils into stockades at night and locked 'em up so they'd know where to find them in the morning. If one of the poor beggars ever escaped, he was nearly always recaptured, brought back and flogged until there wasn't any resistance left in him. Then he was made to work harder then ever in the mine!

"But a day of reckoning finally came — a day when all of the resentment of those proud Indians toward their cruel oppressors was at its highest. They bided their time, planned craftily and on the appointed day took a bloody revenge. The occasion was a fiesta given on a church holiday to celebrate the birth of one of their saints — Saint John the Baptist.

"On Saint John's Day all the converted Apache Indians always gathered at the mission to celebrate the occasion with a grand fiesta and feast. For this memorable occasion the Comanches and their allies came, professing friendship for the priests. They, too, were invited to come to San Saba Mission and have a part in the festival. Very early in the morning of that tragic day, several thousand Indians were gathered around the mission palisades. Lines of Indians reached from Celery Creek, on the east and north, clear up to the old mill above the mission. All the Indians seemed friendly. They said that they had come because the padres had invited them to be there and join in the celebration of the sacred day!

"To forestall any possible treachery, two guards were placed at the entrance gate which was to be opened at nine o'clock. The guards were told to admit only a few visiting Indians at a time. The mission Apaches came first, and after attending Mass, they were sent into the grand patio to make room for others. The visiting tribes outside were begging to be admitted and allowed to receive the sacrament, too.

"At this point a little Apache boy emerged from the shadows. He had often assisted at the altar and was a great favorite with the priests. The boy stealthily approached one of the padres and told him the Comanches were there for no good purpose. They were planning mischief!

"But the priest was an easy-going saint who saw only good in everyone, so the boy's warning went unheeded, and word was passed along

that all visiting Indians were to be admitted
and made welcome. So, after the Comanches
had stacked their side-arms outside the presidio
gate, they were allowed to come in. No one took
the precaution of looking under the blankets of
those haughty chiefs, where many had concealed
scalping knives and tomahawks. Thus scores
of the savages passed the guards and filtered
into the church.

"Suddenly one of the young chiefs stopped
near the mission door and gave a signal! Other
warriors near the gate seized the guards, tomahawked them and threw the gate wide open!

"Then all of the Indians outside the gates
rushed in waving tomahawks or scalping
knives, for they were fully armed. With wild,
blood-curdling war whoops, the savages lost no
time in starting the massacre. The soldiers on
guard, caught by the suddenness of the attack,
were quickly cut down. By noon there wasn't a
white man left alive inside the barracks — not
a living witness to tell the inside story of that
terrible tragedy! The avenging Indians were
determined to make a thorough job of it, so
they took the robes of the holy fathers, the uni-
forms of the soldiers and their guns and ammunition. Everything of value that could be car-

ried away was taken outside the palisaded grounds; then the whole presidio-mission was set on fire and burned to the ground.

"While this was going on, scores of savages, uttering blood-curdling war whoops, struck the post and went directly to the mine. There they destroyed all of the operating equipment and burned everything combustible.

"After the fires had died out, the victorious savages scraped up all the ashes and rubble which had accumulated during the years and dumped it into the open shaft of the mine. On top of this they shoveled in the slack and soil until every trace of the mine was completely destroyed. Thus the once formidable presidio and all that it stood for was completely wiped out!

"Quite satisfied with the damage, the savages next divided the loot, rounded up the mission children and took them away as captives. Still on the warpath, the Comanches hunted down and tomahawked every white settler in the whole San Saba region. Soon the hills were again overgrown by prickly pears and chaparral thickets and became the haunts of buffalo herds, wild mustangs, deer and coyotes. So Liltamilpas, once the 'Summerland' of roving Apaches, now became the hunting grounds of the ruthless Comanches.

"Years after the tragic Saint John's Day massacre, a tall, handsome young man — an Indian — stopped at the Alamo Mission here at Bexar and asked to attend Mass. The priest who received the visitor was impressed by his bearing and general intelligence. He talked with the youth and learned that he was the little Apache altar boy who had carried the warning of Comanche treachery to the easy-going priest at the San Saba Mission on that ill-fated day. It was he who gave the Alamo priest the account of what actually happened there so many years before," concluded Pete.

"That must have been three-quarters of a century ago! Has no recent effort been made to relocate and open that silver mine?" asked Bowie as he knocked the dead ashes from his pipe, got up and took the reins from the black boy who had brought his horse.

"Anyone who tried never came back to tell us how he made out," replied Bauer. "It seems like every bit of interest the Spaniards ever had in that mine died on Saint John's Day seventy-odd years ago when the Comanches burned the mission and holed up the mine."

"Fear and superstition may hold the Spaniards back, but some day an enterprising American will break down all obstacles, relocate and operate that mine — if there really is a mine there," Jim Bowie declared as he mounted his horse, bade his host goodnight and left the smithy.

Under a starlit sky Jim rode down the long street which stretched from Bauer's blacksmith shop toward the inn. The storm had subsided as quickly as it had come up, leaving as reminders the water-soaked ground and a cold, northerly wind. But the story of the lost mine had quickened Jim's pulse and sparked his determination. Right here, within easy reach, lay fabulous wealth — untold riches which could be had for the taking. There was a challenge! What an opportunity for a red-blooded American! Time was of the most importance. Plans must be made at once and put into operation.

Arriving at the hostelry, Jim turned his horse over to a stable boy, entered the inn and joined his brother Rezin in their quarters. The Bowie brothers were extraordinary men who saw eye-to-eye on all important questions. A bond of comradeship and devotion, seldom experienced by men, existed between these brothers.

27

Jovial greetings over, Jim recounted his experiences in the hill counrty and retold the blacksmith's story of the lost Spanish mine somewhere in the San Saba hills. Jim's interest ran high. Rezin said that he, too, had heard tall tales about Spanish mines now completely lost somewhere in those hills. To learn more about the legends he had visited the Lipan Indians, had gone with them on a few buffalo hunts and had contributed generously to their stock pile of venison and other wild game for the tribe.

"Why, down at Baxter's Tavern," Rezin confided, "old-timers never tire of telling intriguing tales about Miranda's discovery of vast stores of bullion concealed in caves found in the rugged uplands."

Pipes glowed and candle flames flickered through long hours that night as the Bowie brothers enthusiastically planned their strategy for finding and developing the lost mine.

"As I see it, Jim," Rezin observed, "there are two clear-cut fields of operation — one is field work, and the other is a matter of record-searching. One of us should ride range over this entire San Saba region — get the lay of the land, spot and explore everything that looks like a cave or

Jim left the smithy and rode toward the inn.

mine opening and get on good terms with the Lipan Indians and their allies, the Apaches. The record-searching can be done only in Mexico City and Saltillo. First we must know for certain that the Spaniards discovered and worked mines in this region, among them the Almagres, the lost mine.

"I can do the field work if you will take over the record-searching. You've had more experience with grandees and court officials than I. What do you say about it?"

"Agreed," said Jim. "We'll start in the morning. Each of us will follow his quest until he accomplishes his purpose. The San Antonio Inn will be our meeting place. I'll return here as soon as I get the facts about our lost mine — the Almagres of the San Sabas."

3

A Trip to Mexico

*B*OWIE arrived in Saltillo at fiesta time. The occasion was the national festival of Mexico, which lasted a week. During this time more gunpowder was wasted, more money gambled away, more music made and more good times displayed than during any other season of the year. In exuberant holiday spirits people gathered from all parts of the Republic to participate in and enjoy the hilarious merry-making.

In the evenings tradespeople and peons danced in the parks under open pavilions and in the streets, in joyous abandon, keeping time to

31

the music of troubadors with banjos, guitars and tambourines.

Many important guests were entertained at court. Jim had influential friends who got invitations for him to attend all state social functions, including the governor's reception and ball.

On the morning of the first day Bowie met his friend Juan Navarro, who greeted him. "Jim, you're just in time. The bullfights are scheduled for this morning. Join me and we'll go to the vice-governor's box in the amphitheater. My sister and her family are expecting me to be with them. Juan Veramendi is detained by a called meeting of governors."

When they arrived at the arena, Navarro and Bowie found their way to the vice-governor's box in the amphitheater, where Mrs. Veramendi and her daughter Ursula were scanning the program for the day's coming events. Juan presented Bowie to his sister and to his niece. The men had arrived at an opportune time; the morning's events had been announced. The first number was scheduled — a bullfight. All eyes were on the arena. The master of ceremonies made the announcement. The matadors were ready, dressed in costumes of satin with gold trimming and making a splendid appearance! Each one would have an opportunity to demonstrate his skill during the day's sports.

Conversation in the Veramendi box became animated. The name of the first challenger for honors was called; he stepped out and took his place in the arena. The pen-gate was opened, and an angry bull came bellowing toward him, head lowered, red nostrils dilated, bloodshot eyes rolling from amphitheater to matador and grizzly tail lashing the air.

The amphitheater rocked with the wild applause of the enthusiastic spectators. One of the matadors wore the Veramendi colors. Ursula pointed this out to Jim, and during the morning she frequently appealed to him for advice on how to keep her score sheet.

The governors' meeting over, Juan Veramendi returned to his box in the amphitheater. Soon afterward Juan Navarro and Bowie, each having made previous engagements, took leave of the ladies after promising to see them again during the week's festivities and to surely attend the Governor's Ball.

The evening of the ball arrived. Jim, faultlessly dressed in fashionable evening clothes, was a distinguished, handsome person, much sought after by titled señors with marriageable señoritas.

As soon as he had formally greeted his host and hostess and had passed down the reception line, Jim sought Ursula and claimed her as his partner for the opening dance. This was a momentous occasion for Bowie. The young girl's beauty, grace and charm held him captive. Before the evening was over he knew that he would declare his love and marry this girl. Ursula knew it, too, before her first dance with him was finished.

But James Bowie would not approach the viceroy of Texas with empty pockets when he declared his love for this charming girl and asked for her hand in marriage.

He, James Bowie, would come as the prospective husband of such a girl should come — with plenty of money, able to maintain for her the same social prestige that she now held! In Texas lay the answer to all of his hopes, the fulfillment of his aspirations.

There was the Almagres, the lost mine of the San Saba hills. He would rediscover and own that mine! Positively nothing would stand in his way of achieving his purpose. Here and in Mexico City he would search the old records; he would have the facts!

When the orchestra stopped for intermission, Jim and Ursula left the ballroom and walked to the patio of the governor's palace. The silver light of the full moon had turned the garden into a fairyland. The air, fragrant with the scent of honeysuckle and magnolia blossoms, carried the plaintive note of a mockingbird calling to her mate.

As they walked, Ursula said, "You came from the States, did you not, Mr. Bowie?"

"Yes, I'm from Louisiana. My name is James — Jim to my friends. You are my friend, aren't you, Señorita Veramendi?"

"I am honored that you want my friendship, Jim, and to you I am Ursula," replied the girl. "How do you like our Texas? Does it have promise enough to keep you here?"

"Do I like your country — your Texas?" breathed Jim. "Texas is magnificent! Her flower-covered hills, fragrant magnolia blossoms and gigantic live oaks that give color and afford shade to the rolling plains where buffaloes herd, wild horses and longhorn cattle graze — your country — your Texas is stupendous! The call of her land is matched only by the beauty and charm of her fair women!

"I am on an important mission now, but when it is finished, I shall return. I love you, darling Ursula, my dearest dear. I have made certain commitments which must be met. When they are fulfilled, I shall return. Will you marry me then — help me establish a home in your glorious state? Ursula, with you to share my life, my all, I can go out and conquer the whole universe! Will you marry me, darling?"

For a long moment the girl stood silently toying with her fan. Then she spoke. "Yes, Jamie, I promise to marry you. I would like to help you found our home in our beautiful Texas. But what is this important mission? May I not help you accomplish that which you seek? My father is viceroy of Texas, you know. He has influence."

"The real work of accomplishment on this project is for me, darling," replied Jim. "When I have established my lines, I will return to you. Then we will go to your father and declare our love. Tomorrow I must be on my way to Mexico City.

"You may have heard legends about rich Spanish mines located somewhere here in Texas,

36

and hidden caverns where vast fortunes of many old Spanish grandees were hidden away for safe-keeping. Then the secret of their locations became lost to the heirs!

"Well, I'm running down recorded information about one of those old, lost Spanish mines. When I get this information and establish my claim to the mine, I shall be free to go to your father. Then we can plan our future.

"Now I shall soon be on my way to Mexico City, there to find and search those old state records. I must discover all that I can about the old Spanish Almagres mine, the lost mine in the San Saba hills.

"As legend has it, this mine, which is thought to contain tremendous wealth, is located in the Lipan Indian territory, in their 'Summerland.' Only a chosen few of these Lipans know the secret of the mine's location, and there is a death penalty declared for any one of them who betrays the secret."

"Oh, how thrilling!" cried Ursula. "Isn't there something I can do to help in this romantic search?"

"A letter of introduction to the right people would be valuable," said Jim. "Can you get such a letter from your father for me? I would appreciate that — but he must not know our secret yet."

"I think I can get the letter for you, Jamie. I'll see father in the morning. I'll also gather all the information about the lost mine, the Almagres, that I can around here. I will have something for you when you come again, Jamie," replied Ursula. "And now we must go back to the salon. Shall we say goodnight here in the patio?"

Holding her in a close embrace, Jim kissed Ursula fervently and whispered, "This, my darling, my love, my own, is a sacred seal of our engagement. I will come back and claim you for my bride before another fiesta rolls around. And now sweetheart, goodnight!"

In Mexico City, Jim found Governor Veramendi's letter of introduction a perfect passport to those in authority. He soon had access to the records of the preceding century. In them he found that in 1756 the viceroy of Mexico had chosen one Don Bernardo de Miranda, then lieutenant general of the Province of Texas. He was to equip himself with such materials and men as he deemed necessary and to thoroughly investigate the mineral resources,

Holding her close, Jim promised he would return.

which were said to be fabulous, in the San Saba and Llano regions.

Jim read that Miranda immediately prepared to carry out his commission, and in February of that year rode out of San Fernando (San Antonio) with sixteen soldiers, five citizens, an Indian interpreter and several peons.

Miranda and his men struck a northwesterly course, followed it for eight days, then halted and pitched camp on the Arroyo San Miguel (Honey Creek), which is a southern tributary of the Rio de los Chamos (Llano River). A mile from Miranda's camp lay the Cerro del Almagres hills.

From this camp General Miranda ranged over the surrounding country. He found a cavern which he named the cave of Saint Joseph of Alcasar. He explored many other caves and prospected farther into the mountains.

As Jim read on he learned that at last, the survey finished and the specimens of ore taken from the caverns securely packed, Miranda's party broke camp and started back to San Antonio. On the homeward trek they met an Apache Indian who was well and favorably known around Bexar. The Indian told General Miranda that there were more and better mines at Los Dos Almagres, near the source of the Colorado River. He said that "those mines yielded pure silver, like the buckles one puts on his shoes."

Miranda was impressed. He offered to give the Indian a red blanket and a hunting knife if he would guide his party to the Almagres mine. But the Indian refused to take the offer, saying, "Some other time I will show you the way. The Comanches are too numerous and too hostile now; some other time you ask me!"

Three weeks from the time Miranda set out with his expedition he was back in San Antonio and dispatched a report of his findings, with recommendations, to the viceroy in Mexico City. This report said in part:

"The mines which are in the Cerro del Almagres hills are so numerous that I guarantee to give every settler of the Province of Texas a full claim. The principal vein is more than two *varas* in width, and in its westward lead appears to be of immeasurable thickness.

"I recommend the immediate establishment of a presidio there and that mines be opened and operated at once, as all of the natural resources required for supporting a settlement are at hand."

So the San Saba presidio-mission had been built as General Don Bernardo Miranda had recommended, and the Almagres mine opened and worked at a profit. Jim, satisfied with what he had learned from the old records, was now ready to return to Texas.

4

A Campfire Agreement

*J*IM had arrived back in San Antonio in time for the fall round-up. He and Rezin had no cattle of their own on range, so they rode herd for Juan Seguin and Juan Navarro. They, with a score of other cowboys, had been trailing longhorns all day. Now, with mess over, they made camp on a cap-rock ledge overlooking the San Saba Valley.

The campfire, made from rosin-packed logs interspersed with cedar boughs, gave off a pleasant, pungent odor. The horses, picketed in a chaparral thicket nearby, had quit milling around and had settled down for the night.

Most of the fellows had lighted their pipes; all were relaxed.

Jim's voice broke the stillness. "Boys," said he, "have you ever thought of this — big money can be cleaned up faster here in Texas than cattle men will ever be able to do it. Right here in these hills there's silver enough to guarantee a brilliant future for every one of us here tonight. Those nuggets the Lipan Indians bring in and barter for supplies are almost pure silver.

"You've all heard about the lost mine in the San Saba hills — the Almagres? Well, she can't be many leagues from right here where we're camped tonight. She's hidden away out there under a blanket of wild flowers and cactus. Her silver can be had by men who have what it takes to go after it. What do you say? Shall we go out and stake our claims?"

Genial Tom McCaslin, running his long fingers through his thick, auburn hair, drawled, "The mine may be out there, as you say, Jim, but how are we goin' to negotiate that little item of capturin' it? You all know the redskins are pretty skittish about white hombres who go prospectin' around the location of the old San Saba Mission site.

44

"They seem to remember that somehow the devotions of the benevolent Fathers got all mixed up with Spanish soldiers who forced the Indians' ancestors to work in that lost mine. Indians who came to the mission to worship got picked up and put into that mine where they had to work moons on end. It sort o' made a lastin' impression on 'em. Old-timers tell me that after the Saint John's Day clean-up, it ain't been at all healthy for white hombres to go out there prospectin' for that old mine.

"As I get it, more than one ambitious hombre, bent on that treasure-hunt, has faded out and left no chart nor blueprint tellin' where his next port-o'-call was goin' to be. I hanker after my share of the silver, if it's to be had, but my ear ain't listenin' for Gabriel's trumpet call askin' me to come up pronto an' help explore heaven. These Texas hills look mighty good to me. But — you understand — I'm no tenderfoot. I'm ready to join up whenever I'm convinced there's a mine out there worth goin' after."

From the other side of the campfire Bob Armstrong called out, "I'm ready to stand by what Tom's just said."

"I'll throw in on them terms, too," agreed Mathew Doyal.

45

"How about the rest of you?" Jim asked.

"Count me in," boomed James Coryell, while the others all joined in a chorus of hearty consent.

"Looks to me like you fellows aren't completely sold on this expedition and won't be until we clear up a couple of counts," said Jim. "You want bona fide proof that there was a paying mine out there. So did I, and I found it in the archives at Mexico City. There in the old records were the confidential, official reports, written in Spanish and sent from the governor of the Province of Texas to the viceroy of Mexico.

"In the first report the Texas governor said that a rich vein of silver ore had been discovered in the vicinity of Los Almagres. He recommended that Don Miranda, then lieutenant general of Texas, be delegated to investigate the area. If the facts came up to the expectations, a presidio was to be founded there and Miranda was to be given the rank of captain and put in command.

"There was no further reference made to the mining project for a score of years. Then Texas had a new governor. He, too, wrote the viceroy about the rich metal-bearing ore found in the

Los Almagres area. He proposed that a strong presidio be founded and a garrison of two hundred soldiers stationed there.

"The report further declared: 'Given this protection, the precious metal can be profitably mined, for the actual fact that the country abounds in numerous rich mines of silver, which offer splendid profit for more than four hundred owners, has been established beyond any reasonable doubt.'

"That, boys, is what I learned from those confidential old reports stored in the archives in Mexico City. As for myself, I now have no doubt that the mine exists. My purpose is to locate that lost mine," Jim concluded, "and by the grace of God and my long rifle, I shall find it!"

5

Gifts for the Chief

THE round-up over, Jim and Rezin saddled
their mustangs and rode out into the San
Saba hills, exploring, scouting and getting
acquainted with the Indians. They used every
clever ruse their ingenious minds could devise to
discover the location of the Almagres mine, but
all to no avail.

They built up friendly relations with the
redskins and circulated freely through the
Lipans' camps. They went on hunting expeditions with Chief Xolic and his warriors and
often shared the shelter of an Indian's tepee.
The Lipans liked the boys and were friendly,

but if either of them asked about the old mission or the mine, he received only cold, suspicious looks and evasive grunts.

Having followed elusive clues for a fortnight, the Bowies, convinced that the trails were all stone-cold, returned to San Antonio. But Jim didn't come back from that expedition beaten. He had charted a course in his own mind, and he would tell no one of it. However, it soon began to unfold.

Chief Xolic had always been friendly toward Jim. Now it was noticed that whenever the old Indian came to Bexar, Jim was on the alert to welcome him and show him some new courtesy.

On one occasion when Xolic rode into town, he found Jim lounging on the platform in front of the trading post, his smartly-equipped sorrel tied at the hitching rack. As the old chief rode up to the store and dismounted, Jim joined him. He ran an appraising eye over the Indian's horse, stroked the arched neck and glistening flanks of the spirited animal, and said, "That's a fine horse you ride, Chief. How fast is he?"

"Him a good horse; goes fast like East Wind. Helps make big medicine when Lipans hunt buffalo. You have nice horse, too. Fine trappings make horse look good."

The alert old Indian stepped up to Jim's filly, moved his hands longingly over the new, creaking leather of the custom-made saddle and let the strong, pliable reins run lightly through his fingers.

Turning abruptly, he pointed to the bale of buffalo hides he had brought in. He then produced two leather pouches filled with lizard-shaped nuggets of silver and placed these on the hides. He squared his shoulders, folded his arms across his breast, looked Jim squarely in the eye and said, "Will my son, Soaring Eagle, trade? I give you buffalo hides and silver for trappings on your horse."

Sober as a judge, Jim examined the proffered buffalo hides, spread them out and counted them. They were beauties; he hefted the pouches of silver. Then he answered: "Those buffalo hides are splendid; the silver nuggets are almost pure metal — but the great Chief, my father, brought them not for me, but to trade for supplies for his people, so I cannot take them. But you make me proud when you call me 'son.' So, if you like my trappings, you shall have them."

Suiting action to his words, Jim stripped the saddle and bridle from his own horse and ad-

Jim revealed a rifle with a silver name-plate.

justed them to the magnificent black stallion which belonged to the old Indian. This done, he rolled up a handsome red and white Mexican *serape* and strapped it on behind the saddle.

Then, turning to lead his own horse down the sun-parched street, Jim said, "There is one thing the great Chief, my father, can do that will make me very glad. It is this: the next time you and your warriors ride the plains to hunt the buffalo, take me with you. I will join in the hunt, and the hides of the buffalo I kill will amply repay me for my gift to you today."

His face passive, but with pride and appreciation glowing in his eyes, the old Indian spoke: "It shall be as you say, my son. When the hunter's moon rides high in the sky, I will come for you. Then we will hunt the buffalo."

A fortnight later Bob Armstrong, Crim Roberts and Jim were at the inn when an Express from New Orleans arrived. The driver delivered a long, sturdily-wrapped package to Jim, who tore away the wrappings and revealed the handsomest silver-mounted long rifle ever brought into Texas. Set in the sturdy ebony stock of the gun was a silver name-plate which bore the inscription: *XOLIC, Chief and High Sachem of THE LIPANS.*

That night Jim took the rifle, with plenty of ammunition, and rode west into the hills. He returned two days later without the gun, but his head was in the clouds. He reined up in front of Roberts' cabin and called out: "Crim, round up the boys. Tell them we'll all meet tonight at Squaw Man's Cove. Sort of a farewell supper," he said whimsically. Then he drew up the slack reins, touched spur to his mustang and was gone.

6

Adoption by the Tribe

CRIM Roberts shoved his sombrero back on his head, thrust his hands deep into his pockets and stood watching Bowie ride out across the trail and disappear in the distance. Ranger, Crim's hound dog, came from the cabin porch, rubbed up against Crim's chaps, bayed and looked up at his master, hoping for an invitation to go on a 'possum hunt.

Crim leaned down, rubbed the hound's ears and said, "Sorry, old pal, but it's no hunting for us today. My work's cut out and I must be on my way. No, sir, Ranger, I never was the squaw-man type of hombre, one always ready to scent out a mystery, but this time Jim's got me guessing. What I want to know is, what did he mean by a 'farewell supper'? Is the man quitting Bexar?

"Well, anyway, I'll ride range today and carry out his orders to round up the boys for a spread at Squaw Man's Cove."

In late afternoon Crim Roberts, back at his cabin, had bathed, shaved and freshened up for the stag party. His mustang, saddled and ready to mount, was staked in a mesquite patch near the cabin. Along the western horizon a lone horseman could be seen approaching at a leisurely lope.

Just at sunset Tom McCaslin reined up at the cabin and hallooed. Crim left his porch, told Ranger to stay at home and take care of the ranch while he was away, mounted his horse, and together the two plainsmen set out for Squaw Man's Cove.

It was a perfect night. A gentle breeze stirred the softly cool Texas air. The hunter's moon, high in the heavens, shone through the foliage of live oaks and made a mackereled pattern on the trail to the rendezvous. As they neared the Cove, they noticed that a pungent odor arose from the burning cedar logs mingled with the delectable aroma of roasting venison and coffee.

One by one the fellows rode in, hobbled their mounts and were soon at ease around the campfire. Light banter, jesting and laughter among the men added relish to the food. The evening wore on. Finally, draining the last tin of coffee from the grounds, Jess Wallace said, "Jim, the chuck was fine, but where do we go from here?"

"That," replied Jim, "brings us down to why I asked all of you to meet here tonight. You remember when we were out on the fall round-up I promised to locate the lost mine of the San Sabas? Since then Rezin and I have combed the countryside and have resorted to every stratagem we could think of to accomplish our purpose, but we've learned nothing.

"I'm convinced that the odds against any white man's learning the secret, and living to profit by it, are too heavy to gamble on. I've asked you here tonight to wish me Godspeed. Tomorrow I leave Bexar a full-fledged Indian — the adopted son of Chief Xolic, a blood brother of the Lipans. I shall never stop until I open the Almagres Mine, the lost mine in the San Saba hills!"

Mounting his horse, Bowie looked up and

56

said, "I go now to join the venerable chief and his warriors who are camped beyond the village on the cliffs." Raising his sombrero, he gave a salute, put spurs to his horse and disappeared into the night.

Jim's declaration of purpose and departure cast a gloom over the party. The change of spirit that came over the fellows was as swift and devastating as the icy blast of a norther sweeping down from the mountains. The boys milled around the fire in moody silence for an hour or more; then, with a show of bluster, one after another caught up his horse and rode away.

Bob Armstrong and Crim Roberts were the last to leave. They stayed to cover the dying embers of the spent fire with ashes; then, mounting their horses, they followed the trail to San Pedro Springs. As they entered a cedar grove on a commanding ridge across the ravine from the springs, the mustangs became nervous. Their necks arched, ears pricked forward, nostrils dilated; they sniffed the air, pranced, pawed the ground and snorted.

The two men quieted their horses and listened. Soon the weird rumble of muffled drum beats reached their ears. It was the tom-toms of the Lipans rolling off a dirge-like march which always accompanied the ceremonial dances of the tribe. The tom-tom beats grew louder; the Indians were approaching. Soon the rhythmical thud of moccasined feet could be plainly heard.

Gradually the blackness of night faded out. The first rich glow from the rising sun suffused the eastern sky. In the early twilight they saw the pageantry of the Indian adoption ceremony.

Nature had set the stage. The actors were finding their places. First came the seasoned warriors, then the younger Lipan braves. All were decked out in tribal regalia. They formed a line at San Pedro Springs. As the tom-tom beats rolled, in slow time, all joined in a monotonous chant. The body of each Indian, bent forward until nearly parallel with the ground, swayed rhythmically; then action commenced.

The stomp, stomp, stomp of moccasined feet falling in unison on the hard earth blended, fluid-like, with the slow drum beats. The Indians were headed for the summit of Saddle Back Mountain. Where the terrain leading to the top of the mesa became more steep, the dancers slowed down almost to a walk. They resembled a company of infantry soldiers at drill. There were no brusque movements.

Flanking the foot dancers came Chief Xolic. He rode his high-stepping black stallion equipped with the splendid outfit Jim had given him. No foreign potentate ever graced a throne with more dignity than the old chief displayed as he sat his horse and presided at that adoption ceremony!

Having reached the flat top of the mesa, the old chief dismounted and stood with his back toward the dancers, facing the eastern horizon. The drone of the tom-toms died away. The chanting and dancing ceased. James Bowie, wearing a tunic of soft, white doeskin and the traditional moccasins of the tribe, stepped out from among the dancers and stood beside the chief.

Grasping Jim's left hand with his right one and raising both toward heaven, Xolic called upon his Father, the Sun; his Mother, the Earth; and the four winds to witness that this man, James Bowie, was henceforth and forever to be his own "blood son" — Soaring Eagle. Then turning to his right, Chief Xolic so declared Jim to his tribesmen.

The ceremony that the two men had just witnessed was finished, and with heavy hearts Bob and Crim turned their mustangs and rode in silence to their cabins.

7

A Good Indian

AT SUNSET Jim, Xolic and the other warriors arrived at the Lipan village where the entire camp was vibrating with excitement. In the old chief's wigwam elaborate plans were in progress for a feast. This was to be followed by a social dance for the entire village.

To accommodate the dancers, two large tepees were pitched close together, side flaps pinned back, making one large room. One tepee was for the men and drums; the other was for the women and dancing. On the men's side half a dozen Indians squatted around a big tom-tom. Each had a wooden drumstick about two feet

60

long which ended in a cotton rag buffer. Each one had his portion of the drum head upon which to beat. All would follow the rhythm of the leader.

When the tom-tom was finally struck, the entire camp assembled; all were dressed in gala attire. The squaws forgot all personal grievances and mingled on equal terms of friendliness and sociability.

None of the guests were met at the entrance or welcomed. The men found their way to the drum room where Chief Xolic and some of his warriors sat smoking. The women, with much chatter and laughter, squatted around the walls of the dancing tepee. A volley of thuds on the drum head announced that the drummers were ready to begin. This was a signal for the squaws to take over and let the drummers know what they wanted for the opening dance.

The squaws chose White Fawn, the old chief's youngest daughter, to be their leader. She was a beautiful maiden, tall and supple, and was a great favorite with everyone. White Fawn came forward and called her choice of a dance number. All of the other squaws stood ranged around the wall of the tepee. The drummers beat out a rhythm, and all began chanting. Gradually the drum beats quickened; the chanting increased in volume and intensity until, with pulses tingling, all feeling of restraint was submerged.

White Fawn went to the center of the floor, danced around the circle alone, then circled back toward Jim. Her limpid eyes rested upon him; she advanced, grasped his hands and triumphantly led him to the center of the dance floor. Arms around each other, they circled the dance floor three times, then separated to choose new partners.

With a look of hatred directed toward Jim, Tres Manos threw his drumstick down and left the tepee. For him the evening's festivities were over; he had one more score to settle with this white imposter when the day of reckoning came!

But back at the tepee the dancing and merry-making continued through most of the night, with Jim and White Fawn partners for each new dance. When all comers were happily tired out, the party broke up. Jim had now established himself and was accepted a "blood brother" in the Lipan tribe.

For eleven months Jim Bowie lived among the Lipan Indians. He entered wholeheartedly into their camp life and daily pursuits. He was an expert buffalo hunter, and in rifle marksmanship he had no equal. He never went to San Antonio, but a half-breed, Trapper Joe, frequently went to the trading post and carried tidings of new Lipan activities.

There were old feuds between the Lipans and their neighbors, the Apaches and Comanches, and Xolic wanted the Lipan losses avenged. So on two occasions the old chief set up the post in the center of the village and declared that his blood son, Soaring Eagle, would lead the Lipans in a foray of vengeance.

Criers, beating tom-toms, were sent through the village calling all warriors and braves to rally to the post. The entire camp quickly responded; a score or more warriors and braves, decked out in war-paint, formed a circle around the post.

Again the tom-toms began to roll. Chanting, all began to sway to the rhythm and to march in single file in an ever-widening circle around the post. Gradually the tempo and fervor of the drum beats increased, and the marchers quickened their steps to crouching bounds, accompanied by wild war whoops. As the excitement increased, each warrior leaped to the post, struck it with his coup stick and gave a glowing description of what he intended to do when he met the enemy. Finally all of the savages caught the spirit, joined the dance and struck the post. On each occasion Tres Manos was the last to fall in line and declare himself.

The first expedition was against the Apaches on the North Concho River. Jim led the attack which ended in a smashing victory for the Lipans. This was quickly followed by another foray against a much larger band of marauding Comanches camped around Pecan Bayou. The town of Brownwood was later laid out on that old Indian battlefield.

On this occasion, too, Jim, joined by Xolic, laid out the plan and strategically led the attack which ended in another Lipan victory. Jim brought back many trophies of valor which gave him even greater prestige as a courageous warrior among his tribesmen.

Each new daring deed increased Jim's popularity with old and young warriors alike, while the old chief's admiration for and pride in his adopted son was boundless.

During the eleven months, Bowie's stewardship in the tribe was so consistently perfect that he was accepted by all as a member of the tribe. His adopted brothers now trusted him completely and led him along a secret passage to the long-coveted mine!

Jim's hopes and expectations had been high, but he had never dreamed of being surrounded by such stupendous wealth as now greeted his eyes! Whether it was a natural vein or smelted bullion was not important; it was a gigantic fortune of rich "Spanish stuff."

Bowie's long quest had suddenly ended successfully. However, he had not been conditioned to deal rationally with such an astounding revelation. The sight of such a fabulous fortune brought about a complete change in the man. His quest for the mine was an accomplished feat, and caution and judgment were thrown to the winds.

Jim, emerging from the mine, was completely convinced that its reputed wealth was not over-estimated. His one overpowering thought was how to gain possession of the cache and claim its magnificent treasure.

8

Return to San Antonio

A SHORT time after learning the Lipans' closely-guarded secret, Jim left the tepee of the old chief. He moved noiselessly out of the sleeping Indian village, saddled his bronco, deserted the tribe and rushed back to San Antonio. As he raced his mustang over wooded hills and across the plains, his plans took form. When he reached the village, he would go first to the inn and find Rezin. Together they would map plans for what should be done, whom they would ask to string along with them, and when they should start.

Jim didn't want too large a group with

66

whom he would have to share his newly-discovered fortune, but he realized that he would need a considerable number of men to beat back and overcome the Indian guardsmen stationed around the mine. He decided it would be best to ask only the fellows who already shared his confidence about the mine, those who already had declared themselves. On those and many other points he needed Rezin's sober advice.

Arriving in San Antonio, Jim found Rezin at the inn and told him he had located the lost mine, and described the magnificent fortune he found cached in it. He estimated the hazards involved in possessing it.

In discussing the whole situation, he said, "As I see it, Rezin, the fortune cached in that lost mine of the San Saba hills is stupendous: it is beyond description! The Indians not only know something of its great value, but also have a superstitious fear that if the mine is ever again worked by white men, they themselves will be persecuted and driven from their tribal hunting ground."

"How do you feel about it yourself, Jim?" asked Rezin. "Are the odds in our favor? Would the benefit be worth the hazard? If you say the word, I'm ready to string along with you; you know that."

"Sure, Rezin, we can overcome all the odds! I haven't spent eleven months with the tribe for nothing. I'm no longer regarded as a white man. I am now an Indian, Soaring Eagle, blood son of Chief Xolic and blood brother of all Lipans!"

So it was agreed that the Bowies would go after the treasure and stake their claim for the lost mine. Plans for the expedition got under way, but it took time to arrange the whole campaign. Meanwhile Trapper Joe came down from the San Saba hills and brought disturbing tidings from Liltamilpas. Old Chief Xolic, grieving deeply over Soaring Eagle's sudden departure, had become ill; an unhealed battle wound flared up. He rallied for a short time only, then died. Tres Manos, who had bided his time, now came forward and declared himself chief of the tribe.

While plans were being made, Jim became impatient to claim Ursula Veramendi for his own. He felt that the lost mine surely would soon be his. He made his way to the Spanish Governor's Palace in San Antonio, where the Veramendis had taken up residence. At the palace, Jim was received joyously by the entire family, for the tall, handsome, purposeful American was a great favorite with them. His previous commitments now fulfilled, Jim went to Vice-governor Veramendi, declared his love for the charming daughter who had captured his heart during the colorful days of the last National Fiesta and asked her hand in marriage.

It was not long until the engagement was announced; the banns were read at the church services in the San Fernando Cathedral. Soon Ursula Veramendi, a descendant from a line of blue-blooded Spanish noblemen, and James Bowie, a planter and aristocrat from Louisiana, were married in a regal ceremony.

They made plans for their future home in beautiful Texas, but they could not proceed too rapidly, for Jim was a very busy man in the months after his return from the San Saba hills.

9

A Fight with Tres Manos

*T*RAPPER Joe, having bartered the last pelts from his season's catch, was leaving the trading post a few days later when he saw Tres Manos with a small bodyguard ride up. He was hunting for Jim Bowie.

When they finally met, the self-appointed Lipan chief taunted Jim, saying, "Why has Soaring Eagle left the camp of his adopted people? Why has he deserted his blood brothers, the Lipans? When old Xolic was our chief, you flattered him with false praise and gave him fine presents. You deceived the simple old man and stole your way into his heart. You made him believe that you thought him a great sachem and a valiant warrior!

"Xolic was a stupid old fool who believed and trusted you. He adopted you as his blood son and brought you to live in his tepee. There you stole the heart of his fair daughter, White Fawn. But you loved them not. You only deceived them. Your purpose in joining the Lipan tribe was to learn the secret of the Indian's hidden mine. When this was accomplished, you quickly deserted the tribe and returned to the palefaces.

"But your trickery will do you no good now, Soaring Eagle, for I, Tres Manos, am now chief of the Lipans. I am warning you and your followers never again to enter our San Saba hunting grounds. If you do, my warriors and I will hunt you down and have your scalps. Remember this, Soaring Eagle. I have spoken!"

It was easy to see Jim's Scotch-Celtic temper was up. When he spoke, his answer was a bristling challenge. He taunted the arrogant Indian who pompously sat on his horse by saying, "Tres Manos is no warrior. He is a squaw who hides his cowardice by idly blustering. He hopes to make himself powerful in the camp of my brothers, the Lipans, by blackening the rep-

71

utation of their noble chief, Xolic, my father, and the fair name of his gentle daughter, White Fawn, my sister.

"I lived in my father's wigwam and loved him. I did not learn from him or from White Fawn any secret that was not revealed in tribal ceremony. I am a Lipan Indian, blood son of our venerable Chief Xolic, and will defend his honorable name.

"You are no chief, Tres Manos! You are only a yelping coyote! It was a sorry day for my adopted tribesmen when they allowed you to become their chief. You cannot defend Liltamilpas, the tribal hunting grounds, or protect the tribe from danger, because you have a cowardly heart. You dare not doff your trappings and defend yourself now!"

As Jim finished speaking, he snatched off his sombrero, advanced and struck Tres Manos across the face. In a black rage the infuriated Indian leaped from his horse, threw off his blanket and war bonnet and with an ear-splitting whoop, sprang at Jim.

They met in combat and for some moments fought with equal strength and skill. Then backing away for a split second, the savage crouched, leaped through the air and caught

Tres Manos caught Jim in the chest with his head.

Jim in the chest with his head. They went down together! When they hit the ground, Tres Manos, on top, had Bowie pinned to the ground — but not for long!

With a quick surge of power Jim freed his arms and stood off the Indian with counter-punches. Finally a well-aimed undercut to the jaw knocked Tres Manos out. Jim was instantly astride the redskin's prostrate body, holding the inert, dust-caked form in a vise-like grip between his knees. Bowie slapped the savage's unresisting head from side to side.

Fearing that the helpless warrior would be killed, Rezin and Juan Navarro stepped in and pulled Jim away from the limp form of the hapless Lipan chieftain.

The hostile Indian, laid low in San Antonio's dusty street, made no effort to get up. Silently and sullenly his followers came forward to help their beaten and humiliated chieftain onto his horse. So the Lipans' war party, which had ridden into Bexar so pompously, hunting for Jim Bowie, departed for their hunting grounds in the San Saba hills, crestfallen and dejected.

After the Tres Manos episode was made known, a new interest in the lost mine swept over Bexar. Every able-bodied man in the colony wanted to join a volunteer squad, with Bowie as leader, to go directly to the old San Saba mission-presidio site and take possession of the mine. Thirty-four signed up for the venture, but when all arrangements had been made and the time came to start, the number had dwindled to ten men and two servant boys.

10

A Search for the Mine

ON November 2 the adventurers set out from San Antonio on the seventy-league trek, as fearless and undaunted a group of young Anglo-Americans as ever stepped out on Texas soil. Those in the party were James and Rezin Bowie, Dave Buchanan, Cephas Hamm, Mathew Doyal, Tom McCaslin, Bob Armstrong, James Coryell, Jesse Wallace, Crim Roberts, two servant boys, Gonzales, a Mexican peon and Jim's servant boy, Charley.

It was Jim's declared intentions to go directly to San Saba and build a stockade on the site of the old mission-presidio. This would serve as headquarters and as protection against the Indians while they re-opened and worked the mine. The men had an ample supply of arms, ammunition, food staples and the necessary implements they would need to open up and operate the mine.

All the travelers were well-mounted, and each had from one to four pack animals to carry food and other equipment. They traveled in the general direction of the old San Saba Mission site for seventeen days, leisurely investigating all known leads for other prospective mines. The trip to this point was uneventful.

On November 19 they crossed the Llano River at the falls and followed the valley up to the present site of Mason. They found a spring of splendid water there and spread camp for the night. Shortly after a campfire had been started, a party of sixteen friendly Indians hailed them.

They said that Tres Manos was on the warpath. "Right now," they continued, "the Lipan chief, with a band of two hundred warriors and braves, is ranging across country to cut you off. They started from Liltamilpas hunting for you and are now headed toward San Antonio."

The Indians advised the men to turn back before it was too late, because they were hopelessly outnumbered and would certainly all be scalped before they could reach the shelter of the crumbling old presidio. But Jim Bowie was not the man to swerve from his purpose or turn his back on any danger, no matter what the odds against him might be. In this case he ran true to form.

The Indian friends received Jim's presents of tobacco and gunpowder graciously and offered to go with them if they would return to San Antonio; but when Jim refused, the Indians wished them well and were soon on their way. Jim saw that the men banked out the campfire early that night, put two men on guard duty, spread a blanket near the horses and turned in for a few hours of rest.

The men broke camp the following morning before sunrise and followed their course toward the site of the old San Sabá Mission, hoping to reach the demolished old fort before dark. Jim and Rezin were in the lead and followed an old buffalo trail for about twelve miles which brought them to another good watering place — the well-known landmark known as Rock Springs.

They nooned there, rested their horses, had lunch, then continued on their way. They had gone about two miles when they came in full view of the Indians who, it seemed, had been warned of their approach and were lined up in battle array ready to give a warm reception.

When Jim first spotted the savages they were nearly a mile away. He cased his field glass, wheeled his horse around and called the men in a huddle.

"Boys," said he, "someone has tipped Tres Manos off. He has his warriors waiting for us. They are all lined up in battle array not a mile from where we are right now. The wily chief has spread his warriors directly across our route, and there isn't a single protective tree in sight.

"It's sure suicide to ride into their ambush and risk an open fight against such heavy odds. But there is still time for us to change our course, which we will do."

He gave the order: "All hands fall in! Rezin will ride as rear guard!"

Jim mounted his horse, rode back to the head of the line and turned due north. The rest followed. Tres Manos kept his warriors in position until the men passed out of sight. He made no move to molest them, but Jim was not deceived by this show of indifference. He knew that danger lurked in the oncoming darkness, that he and his men would be attacked and wiped out during the night unless he could counter-maneuver the crafty chief. But Jim Bowie was a winner; every man in the outfit had confidence in his ability to handle even this situation.

So the little cavalcade stretched out on the new course. The servant boys and the pack horses followed Jim and seven or eight of the men, while the rest, with Rezin, formed the rear guard.

The trail, covered with loose rock fragments and overgrown by underbrush, made traveling difficult. The horses, too, were no longer in prime condition; their hoofs were worn down and broken. There was no mistaking it — the fellows were keenly disappointed, for every jack-man realized that they could not reach the old San Saba mission-presidio ruins that night. They would have to shift as best they could for an advantageous camp site somewhere else.

At sunset the group drew up along the San Saba River near the mouth of Calf Creek, spread camp, cared for the horses, prepared and ate the evening meal. There was no moonlight that night to either help or hinder the situation. When it was pitch dark the boys crept out, one at a time; each man mounted his horse, secured his pack animals and stole silently away. The campfires were left burning.

11

The Calf Creek Battle

JIM was in the lead. He followed Calf Creek upstream about three miles. There he discovered a grove of forty or fifty large live oak trees — like an oasis in the desert — flanked on the north by a thicket of slim oak saplings about ten feet high. This thicket, forty yards long by about twenty yards deep, was surrounded by rock-covered, broken prairie, studded over here and there with a few trees.

A spring-fed stream of sparkling water ran thirty yards west of the live oak grove, which Jim had chosen for a camp. As a precautionary measure, a road was cut ten feet inside the outer edge and completely around the thicket. That finished, the men cleared away the prickly pears, hobbled the horses, placed pickets on guard, rolled into blankets and went to sleep.

Nothing happened during the night. The following morning they were up early and made all possible haste to break camp and be on the way. Jim hoped to cover the last six leagues to the old fort before their position was discovered. They had breakfasted on hardtack and jerked venison and were in their saddles ready to start when the sentry then on duty rushed in with his report:

"Boys, hold everything. You can't go now. I was just finishing a scouting trip out below the thicket when I saw a crouching figure, face near the ground, loping toward our camp. When I sighted the figure first through the gray twilight, I thought it was a prairie wolf, but as it came closer, the form took shape — it was an Indian scout tracking us down!"

Before the sentry had finished speaking, the cries of "Indians!" and "All men to arms!" rang through the camp. Every man quickly dismounted, tied his mount and pack animals to trees, secured his arms and stood ready to defend himself.

83

Tres Manos and his horde of painted warriors were following about fifty yards behind their scout. When they found that the sentry had discovered them, the Indians halted, gave a war whoop and commenced to strip for combat.

A group of redskins was examining the land between the encampment and the stand taken by Tres Manos and the main body of his warriors. Among them were a number of Caddo Indians who had always been friendly to the whites. Since Jim's men were so greatly outnumbered — two hundred of the savages to ten white men — it was agreed that Rezin Bowie, who had volunteered for the job, should go out, talk to the Caddos and find out if some sort of compromise could be agreed upon.

Dave Buchanan pressed forward and offered to go with Rezin. The boys left the shelter of the camp and walked to within a hundred feet of where the Caddos had stopped. Rezin, speaking in their own language, said, "Where is your chief? I want to talk to him. Bring him here."

Speaking in English, the Caddo spokesman answered, "How do you do! How do you do!"

84

He then fired twelve shots; one of them broke Buchanan's leg! Rezin replied to this outrage by firing both barrels of his shotgun and emptying the magazine of his pistol. This done, he took Dave over his shoulder and started back to camp. The Indians again opened fire and gave Buchanan two more flesh wounds. Flying bullets pierced Rezin's hunting shirt in several places but caused no injury to his body.

The savages had failed to stop Rezin with bullets; now eight of them started in pursuit, brandishing their tomahawks and yelling fiendishly. Rezin, refusing to leave Buchanan, was running a losing race; the savages were just closing in when four of the men witnessed the scene and rushed to the rescue; they opened fire and brought down four Indians. The others turned quickly and lost no time in gaining the shelter of their own camp.

When Rezin and Dave reached the shelter of the live oak grove, the men held a hasty council of war. For five minutes everything was quiet; but the quiet was soon shattered by savage war whoops coming from a hill sixty yards to the northeast. There were forty or fifty Indians, armed with rifles, milling around for position. Their chief, perfectly composed, sat on his mustang arrogantly and in a loud, menacing voice urged the savages to charge.

When Jim discovered the chief, he called out, "Who is loaded?"

Ceph Hamm replied, "I am!"

"Shoot that Indian on horseback," cried Jim.

Hamm fired, broke the Indian's leg and killed his horse. Undaunted, the crippled chief adjusted his shield to ward off the bullets and tried to gain shelter behind the dead body of his horse. Four of Bowie's men, having reloaded, fired at the shield, every bullet reaching its target. The wounded chief dropped prone alongside his fallen pony; he was immediately surrounded by six or eight of his followers. They retrieved the wounded body of their fallen chief and carried it away.

"That," said Jim, "was the visiting Caddos' chief!"

His men rapidly reloaded their guns and fired in relays. The heavy barrage from the grove soon drove the savages over the crest of the hill out of rifle range. But they re-formed their ranks and were soon joined by a squad of expert bow-men. With deafening whoops they swarmed down the hill, directing a heavy fire of rifle balls and arrows at Bowie's position. His small band answered with well-directed rifle-fire.

12

The Last Fight

WITH his war bonnet streaming back in the wind, mounted on a Bayo coyote mustang, another arrogant chief came riding like the wind and took up his position on the hill where the first chief had fallen.

Again Jim shouted, "Who is loaded?" There was a dead silence. Every gun was empty! Suddenly Jim's little servant boy, Charley, came racing down with Dave Buchanan's rifle which hadn't been fired since Dave was wounded at early dawn. He held the gun out. Jim took it and fired. Instantly the second chief lurched in his saddle and fell from his horse.

"That was Tres Manos, the self-appointed chief of the Lipan tribe, a poor successor to the venerable Xolic!" Jim remarked caustically as he reloaded the rifle.

While the men had been busily engaged in defending their position against the Indians on the hill, a squad of Caddos had entrenched themselves under cover of the creek bank about forty yards behind them. In a surprise attack they now opened fire and hit Mathew Doyal. He fell, wounded. As he went down, Tom Mc-Caslin rushed up shouting, "Where's the Indian who shot Doyal?"

Everyone realized the Caddos were trained riflemen and yelled at Tom to keep under cover. But, too late! Tom had sighted an Indian and, while in the act of raising his rifle, another redskin shot him through the heart!

Bob Armstrong, who saw McCaslin fall, came loping up bellowing, "Blast the Indian who shot McCaslin! Where is he?"

Crim yelled at Bob to keep back, but he had sighted another Indian, and while bringing his rifle into position, he was fired at, too, the ball lodging against the barrel of his rifle.

So the battle raged on. Soon the grove was completely surrounded by yelling savages who were trying desperately to close in on Bowie. The trees did not afford adequate protection so all the men made a dash for the thicket where their movements were concealed. There they had a distinct advantage, for, by using the road they had cut the night before, they could easily move about, guarding their position from every side.

The Caddos were now in easy rifle range along the creek bank. The men kept them covered, and as soon as one of them raised his head to look around, they had him spotted and picked him off.

The scrimmage lasted for two hours; the Indians were getting the worst of it. With every round of rifle-fire from the guns, six or eight of the redskins went down. Baffled and infuriated by their heavy losses, they at last determined to burn out Bowie and the rest. They set fire to the dry prairie grass. The breeze swept the flames along Calf Creek; there the fire veered to the right and to the left, but left about five acres around the encampment untouched.

During the shank of the afternoon there came a lull in the battle. Not a savage could be seen within rifle range. The hot, murky air was stifling. The men, who had been engaged in active combat for hours, were tired and thirsty. Rezin called for volunteers to go with him to the spring for water; four of the fellows came up with buckets, ready to go. The trip was quickly and successfully made.

Under cover of the darkness caused by the smoke clouds which banked over the terrain in the wake of the prairie fires, the Indians began to carry their dead and wounded comrades off the battlefield. While they were busy doing this, Bowie's boys took stock of their own position and commenced scraping and digging away all of the dry grass and leaves from around the wounded men and the baggage.

They then threw up a rude breastwork of loose rock and green brush around the clearing. They did this as a protection in case the savages eventually fired their position.

When the smoke cleared away and the savages saw they had not succeeded in burning the white men out, they took up their former positions behind rocks and trees. They then commenced another series of attacks which lasted for hours. The two servant boys were kept busy scraping up the dead grass and dry leaves to prevent the fire from spreading within the thicket. The men were constantly on the alert to see that the enemy had no chance to fire the five-acre plot around their position.

Finally the wind shifted to the northeast; the breeze stiffened to a gale. Down along the creek bank an Indian was sighted stealthily setting fire to the dry grass that still surrounded the camp. It was Bob Armstrong who discovered the redskin; he fired and killed the savage before he could get away.

The situation was now a desperate one. The fire, swept onward by the gale, surged toward the camp in billowing waves ten feet or more high. If caught by this onrushing blast, the men would surely be burned to death! However, the Indians' war whoops and the incessant rifle fire from their ambushed position kept the group from leaving the thicket. After a hasty consultation, they decided to stay where they were and fight it out.

When the savages charged, they would give them the contents of their guns, place their backs together, draw knives and fight them as long as any one of them lived.

Then the fire struck the thicket! Every able-bodied man fought it with buffalo robes, bear skins, deer skins and blankets until it was finally under control. They were safe but the thicket was a shambles! It was burned so badly that it now afforded little protection.

All of the men hurried to the clearing where they had earlier thrown up fortifications around their wounded men and baggage. There they began feverishly building the breastworks higher, throwing in loose rock from the inside and chinking in with dirt dug up with hunting knives.

Down in Texas it is generally conceded that the Battle of Calf Creek was perhaps the most heroic and courageously-contested engagement ever fought and won within the borders.

Here Jim Bowie, with a little company of ten men, caught on the open plains without any prearranged fortifications, fought and routed one hundred and sixty-four well-armed Indian warriors who were led by a chief fired with a spirit of personal hatred, seeking revenge. Jim's little company gave the savages such a beating that, counting the battle lost, the redskins withdrew from the field and mournfully lamented their dead throughout the night, but made no further effort to molest the small band of Americans.

In that terrific battle, which lasted all day, there were fifteen infuriated, hostile Indians against each one of Bowie's men. The sparks from battle in their own camp flew so thick and fast that they were in constant danger of having powder horns explode when they uncorked them to reload their guns. The losses of the day stood at one man killed, three injured. The Indians had fifty warriors killed, and thirty-five seriously injured.

Taking inventory of their camp, the courageous men found but few remaining horses, and they were in no condition for immediate travel. Also, something had to be done to relieve the congestion in Dave Buchanan's bullet-shattered leg. The company was without surgical instruments of any kind.

So, resorting to Indian-frontier remedies, they gathered green bark stripped from live oak saplings and boiled it down until the liquid was very strong. Into it they stirred powdered charcoal and corn meal until the mixture became thick; using the mixture for a poultice, they bandaged it around Dave's wounded leg, then sewed a piece of buffalo hide around the bandage.

Jim realized that it would require more

men to carry out his original plan, and although Buchanan's injured leg was healing rapidly, it would be days before he could travel. So Jim decided to stay on in camp and give all of the men and horses some needed and well-earned rest.

During the days that followed, Jim delegated volunteers to go out on daily scouting and exploratory missions. On one of these scouting expeditions Rezin Bowie discovered an interesting cave. It was located in the side of a San Saba range not far from where the Indians had buried their dead warriors after the Calf Creek battle.

The mouth of the cavern was well-concealed by a thicket of chaparral and prickly pears. Inside the cave, a short distance from the entrance and concealed behind a pile of rocks, was a gaping void. In describing it later, Cephas Hamm said, "Rezin explored the opening in the cavern floor and found it to be an entrance to an open mine shaft, about eight feet deep. He improvised a ladder by hacking footholds in a live oak log and descended. He was in an open mine. Using his tomahawk, he hacked off pieces of ore which, when assayed later, turned out to be very rich in silver."

After a week of rest, Jim's men were all anxious to break camp; so they buried their tools, destroyed all excess baggage and prepared for the return trip.

In the evening of the eighth day after the battle, as darkness settled down over the prairies, they left the little improvised fort, traveled all night and until late in the afternoon of the following day. They made camp at a good spring and planned for an early start the following day. They all had expected the Indians to lie in wait for them, but saw no more of them.

Nine days later the company was back in San Antonio. Mexico was undergoing another revolution, and the Anglo-American colonies were seething with unrest. Delegates from all of the colonies were gathered in called conventions where, solidly united, they pledged themselves ready to promote and prepare for home defense against Santa Anna and his Mexican army.

Thus all personal ambition for opening the coveted mine was forgotten — temporarily, it was thought. Every man in Jim's party volunteered to fight, if need be, for Texas and her freedom!

The Bowie brothers, James and Rezin, were among the first to reach Gonzales, where they participated in the first battle of the Texas Revolution. After this battle Jim volunteered to serve in Austin's army and marched with him to a camp near San Antonio. From that camp Bowie led the charge at Concepcion in the so-called Grass Fight.

This skirmish was brought about by the rumor that an approaching burro train carried silver to pay the Mexican garrison stationed at Bexar. But when captured, the burros' packs proved to be only hay sent to feed Ugartechea's cavalry horses!

On December 4 Jim Bowie volunteered "to go with old Ben Milam into San Antonio." Leading a detachment of three hundred volunteers, Ben Milam entered San Antonio the following morning. He stormed the Alamo, and five days later General Cos surrendered and marched his army out of Bexar. But "glorious old Ben Milam" paid with his life for the victory.

Three months later, March 6, 1836, like a rocket through the heavens, James Bowie's spectacular and courageous life ended. Sharing with Travis the defense of the Alamo, he and a hundred and eighty-six others died gallantly, leaving "not one messenger of defeat." His name, with theirs, has become immortal.

But when James Bowie died in the Alamo, he carried with him what many Texans believe to be a "secret as cogent to keep his memory green in the hearts of his countrymen" as was his dramatic part in securing the independence of Texas; for it is commonly believed that Bowie died knowing the location of fabulous wealth.

The mine he sought, and which thousands of people believed he found, was named *Bowie's Lost Mine*. Through the years, even down to the present day, the search for the lost mine goes on. Does Jim Bowie's restless spirit stimulate the treasure-hunt? *Quien sabe?*